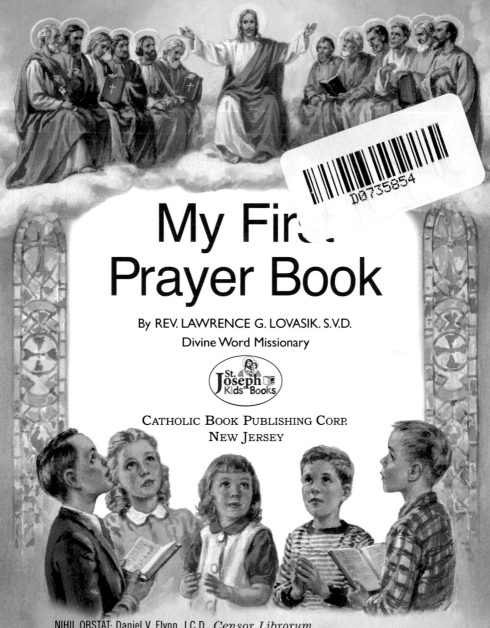

My First Prayer Book

By REV. LAWRENCE G. LOVASIK. S.V.D.

Divine Word Missionary

St. Joseph Kids' Books

CATHOLIC BOOK PUBLISHING CORP.
NEW JERSEY

NIHIL OBSTAT: Daniel V. Flynn, J.C.D., *Censor Librorum*
IMPRIMATUR: Joseph T. O'Keefe, *Vicar General, Archdiocese of New York*

THE OUR FATHER

OUR Father, Who art in
heaven,
hallowed be Thy name;
Thy kingdom come,
Thy will be done
on earth as it is in heaven.
Give us this day our daily bread,
and forgive us our trespasses,
as we forgive those who trespass
against us;
and lead us not into temptation,
but deliver us from evil.
Amen.

THE HAIL MARY

HAIL Mary, full of grace!
The Lord is with thee;
blessed art thou among women,
and blessed is the fruit
of thy womb, Jesus.

Holy Mary,
Mother of God,
pray for us sinners,
now and at the hour
of our death. Amen.

TO THE HOLY TRINITY

G LORY be to the Father,
and to the Son,
and to the Holy Spirit.

As it was in the beginning,
is now, and ever shall be,
world without end. Amen.

THE APOSTLES' CREED

I BELIEVE in **God,
the Father** Almighty,
Creator of heaven and earth,
and in **Jesus Christ,** His only Son, our Lord,

At the words that follow, up to and including the Virgin Mary, *all bow.*

Who was conceived by the Holy Spirit,
born of the Virgin Mary,
suffered under Pontius Pilate,
was crucified, died and was buried;
He descended into hell;
on the third day He rose again from the dead;
He ascended into heaven,
and is seated at the right hand of God
   the Father Almighty;
from there He will come to judge
   the living and the dead.

I believe in the **Holy Spirit,**
the holy catholic Church,
the communion of saints,
the forgiveness of sins,
the resurrection of the body,
and life everlasting. Amen.

5

ACT OF **FAITH**

O MY God, I believe
that You are one God
in three Divine Persons,
Father, Son, and Holy Spirit.
I believe all the truths
the Catholic Church teaches,
because You made them
known to me.

ACT OF **HOPE**

O MY God, I hope in You
because You are all-good
and can do all things.

I hope You will forgive my sins,
and help me with Your grace.

ACT OF **LOVE**

O MY God, I love You with
my whole heart and soul,
because You are all-good.

I love my neighbor as myself
for love of You.

PRAYER TO BE
SORRY
FOR SIN

My GOD,
I am sorry for my sins
with all my heart.

In choosing to do wrong
and failing to do good,
I have sinned against You.

I firmly intend, with Your help,
to do penance, to sin no more,
and to avoid whatever leads me to sin.

MORNING PRAYERS

COME, Holy Spirit,
help me to say
my prayers well.

O Blessed Trinity,
I believe in You,
I hope in You, I love You,
I adore You.

O MY God,
I offer You through the
Immaculate Heart of Mary,
all my thoughts, words, actions,
and sufferings of this day,
to please You, to honor You,
and to make up for my sins.

Sweet Mother Mary,
keep me in your care.

O VIRGIN Mother Mary,
help me to heaven above.
Mother of Jesus, keep me
always as your loving child.

NIGHT PRAYERS

MY GOD and Father,
   I thank You for
all the blessings
   You have given me today.

I am sorry for all my sins,
   because they have hurt You,
   my dearest Father.

Forgive me, O God, and help me
never to offend You again.

Have mercy on poor sinners
and all who need Your help.

Bless my father and mother,
my brothers, sisters and friends.

In Your name, O God,
I go to sleep this night.

My dear Mother Mary,
help me to love God more
and keep me from every sin.

My Guardian
Angel,
help me.

Jesus, Mary,
Joseph!

PRAYER TO
THE INFANT JESUS

DEAR little Infant Jesus,
   I thank You
for leaving heaven
to become a Child like me.

I want to be like You —
   kind and pure and good.
Always be my Friend
   and keep my soul from sin.

Bless my mother and father,
   my brothers and sisters, too.

Bless all who are good to me,
   and all who are in need.

Jesus, Infant Savior,
   give peace to the world!

PRAYER TO
THE HOLY FAMILY

JESUS, Mary's Son, I love You
with all my heart and soul.

Mary, lead me to Jesus,
and make me love Him more.

Joseph, keep me from all evil
and always in your care.

Jesus, Mary and Joseph,
I give you my heart and soul.

I pray, O Holy Family,
bless our family, too,
that we may live as you did —
In God's peace and love.

And when this life is over,
Jesus, Mary and Joseph,
take us to heaven with you.

PRAYER TO
THE BOY JESUS

JESUS, as a boy of twelve,
  You found joy in the temple,
  praying and talking about God.

Help me to learn my Catechism
  and to know more about God.

When You left the temple
  with Mary and Joseph,
  You obeyed them in everything.

Help me to obey my parents,
  the priests and my teachers.

Help me to be more like You
  in all I think or do or say, so
  that I may always please God.

Jesus, friend of children,
  bless all children everywhere.

PRAYER TO SAINT JOSEPH

GOOD Saint Joseph,
I honor and love you
as the foster father of Jesus,
pure husband of Mary,
and head of the Holy Family.

Make my heart pure and fill it
with love for Jesus and Mary.

Be the head of our family
and lead us close to God.

O Saint Joseph, give us peace
and heavenly blessings
and, above all, love.

Saint Joseph, be with us
when we need you most —
may we die as you did,
in the arms of Jesus and Mary.

Through your prayers may we
come to heaven to be
with God and you forever.

PRAYER TO JESUS MY TEACHER

DEAR Jesus, my Teacher,
    You are the Way,
  the Truth and the Life.

  Teach me the truths
  You have given
  to Your Church.

Fill my soul with Your grace
    that I may love God above all,
    and my neighbor as myself.

For You I want to obey
    my parents and teachers
    who take Your place.

Jesus, the Friend of children,
    bless me and the children
    of the whole world.

PRAYER
BEFORE A CRUCIFIX

LOOK down on me,
good and gentle Jesus,
while I kneel here.

Make my soul strong in
faith, hope and love.

Make me really sorry
for all my sins so I
will never sin again.

I am sad
when I see the wounds
on Your hands and feet,
and think of the words
of Your prophet, David:
"They have pierced my
hands and my feet."

Lord Jesus Crucified,
have mercy on us!

PRAYER TO THE
SACRED HEART OF JESUS

MOST Sacred Heart of Jesus,
have mercy on us.

Sweet Heart of Jesus,
I put my trust in You.

PRAYER TO THE
IMMACULATE HEART OF MARY

MOST Pure Heart of Mary,
keep my heart free from sin.

Sweet Heart of Mary,
be my salvation.

HAIL, HOLY QUEEN

HAIL, holy Queen, Mother of mercy;
hail our life, our sweetness,
and our hope.

To you do we cry,
poor banished children of Eve,

To you do we send up our sighs,
mourning and weeping in this valley of tears.

Turn then, most gracious Advocate,
your eyes of mercy toward us.

And after this our exile show unto us
the blessed fruit of your womb, Jesus.

O clement,
O loving,
O sweet Virgin Mary.

PRAYER TO THE IMMACULATE CONCEPTION

O MARY, Mother of Jesus,
   and my dear Mother, too,
I honor and love you
as the Immaculate Conception.

Your soul is most beautiful
   because it is full of grace
   and free from every sin.

Mary, Mother most pure,
   into your care I give
   my body and my soul;
   keep them pure and holy.

O Mary, conceived without sin,
   pray for us
   who have recourse to you!

PRAYER TO MY GUARDIAN ANGEL

ANGEL of God,
my Guardian dear,
God's love for me
has sent you here.

Ever this day
be at my side,
to light and guard,
to rule and guide.

MY dear Guardian Angel,
teach me to know God,
to love and serve Him
and save my soul.

Keep me from all danger,
and lead me to heaven.

PRAYER FOR MY FRIENDS

JESUS, when I am playing
with other boys and girls,
help me to remember how
You played as a Child.

Help me to make my playmates
happy in our games,
because You have taught me
to love my neighbor as myself.

Jesus, bless my friends!